CW01467466

A BIG THANKS TO ALL THE AMAZING AND INSPIRING GARDENERS I'VE EVER MET. HAPPY GROWING TO ALL NEW ONES – BE PATIENT AND REMEMBER THINGS MIGHT NOT ALWAYS WORK THE FIRST TIME ROUND! – M.H.

TO RAFAL, JULEK AND TYTUS WHO ARE CREATING OUR AMAZING GARDEN WITH ME. – M.D.

BIG PICTURE PRESS

First published in the UK in 2024 by Big Picture Press,
an imprint of Bonnier Books UK
4th Floor, Victoria House
Bloomsbury Square, London WC1B 4DA
Owned by Bonnier Books
Sveavägen 56, Stockholm, Sweden
www.bonnierbooks.co.uk

Text copyright © 2024 by Michael Holland
Illustration copyright © 2024 by Maria Dek
Published by arrangement with Debbie Bibo Agency
Design copyright © 2024 by Big Picture Press

1 3 5 7 9 10 8 6 4 2

All rights reserved

ISBN 978-1-80078-603-5

This book was typeset in Ranch Hand and Menco
The illustrations were painted in gouache

Edited by Isobel Boston
Designed by Olivia Cook
Production by Neil Randles

Printed in China

Safety note: We advise that all activities undertaken in this book are completed with adult supervision.

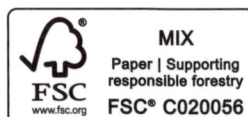

FSC
www.fsc.org
MIX
Paper | Supporting
responsible forestry
FSC® C020056

THE LITTLE GARDENER'S HANDBOOK

MICHAEL HOLLAND

MARIA DEK

BPP

CONTENTS

LET'S GROW FRUIT AND VEG!

LET'S GROW PLANTS!

WELCOME TO THE WONDERFUL WORLD OF GARDENING!

Whether you have a big garden or a small windowsill, you can make the world a greener place. Gardening is one of the best hobbies in the world and it's good for you, your neighbourhood and our planet! People have been gardening in one way or another for thousands of years, so you will be continuing a very long and important tradition.

In this book, you'll learn about how plants work, how to grow your own flowers and vegetables, how to encourage wildlife to your garden and why protecting plants is important for our lovely planet. Along the way, there will be plenty of activities and experiments for you to try for yourself – mostly using everyday materials you can find at home.

What are you waiting for? Let's begin!

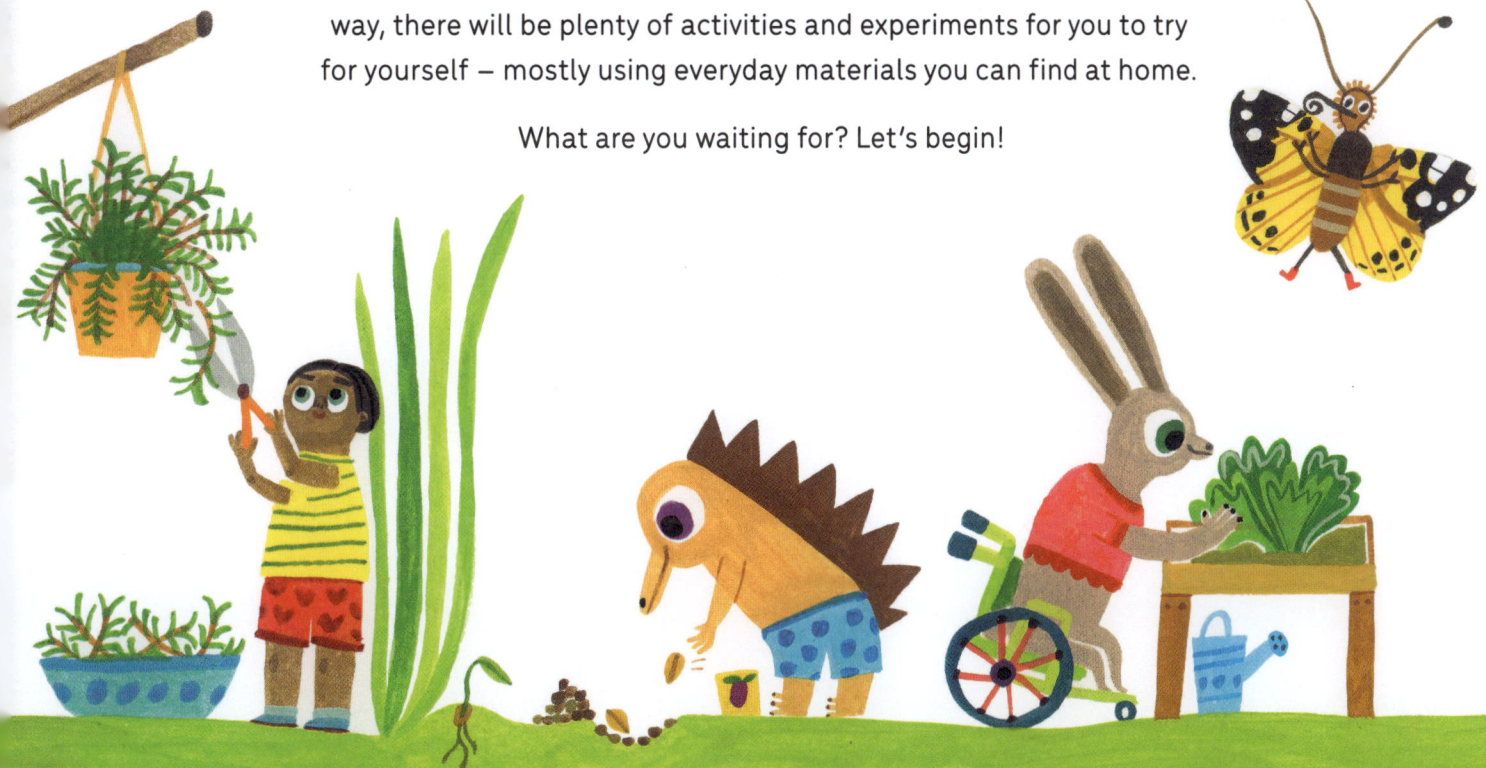

ALL ABOUT PLANTS

WHAT IS A PLANT?

Plants are living things that can be found all around the world. No matter what their shape or size, plants almost always have the same basic parts – **roots**, a **stem**, **leaves** and sometimes **flowers**. Each part of the plant has a very important job to perform.

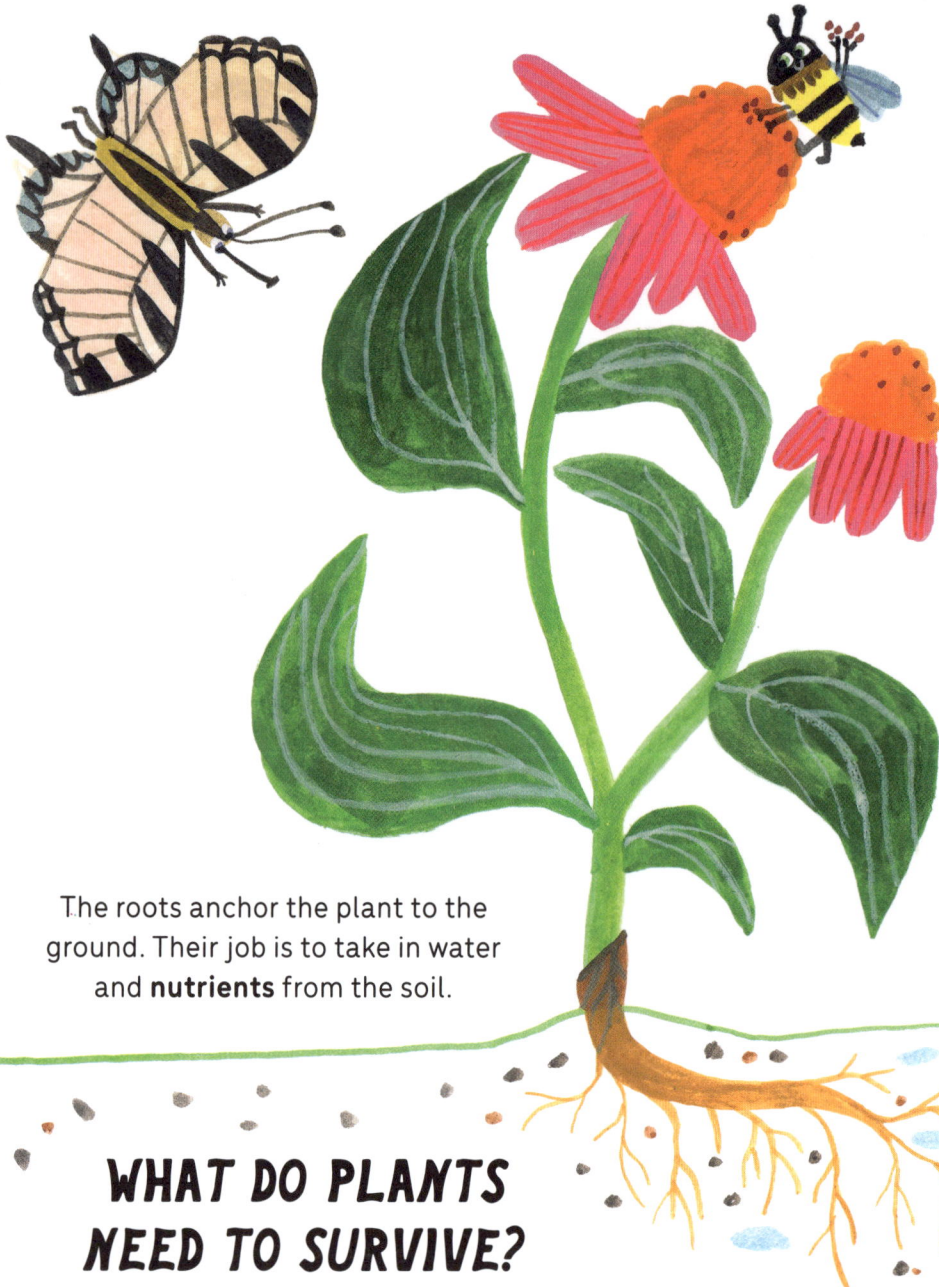

Many plants have colourful flowers to attract **insects**. Flowers produce **seeds** that grow into new plants.

The roots anchor the plant to the ground. Their job is to take in water and **nutrients** from the soil.

WHAT DO PLANTS NEED TO SURVIVE?

AIR

Plants need air to make food and to breathe. During the day, plants absorb a gas called **carbon dioxide** from the air and they release a gas called **oxygen** (the gas we need to survive).

SUNLIGHT

Plants are able to create their own food using sunlight. Leaves are designed to absorb energy from the sunlight and they use this to convert water and carbon dioxide into special plant food. This amazing process is called **photosynthesis**.

Plants need sunlight to stay alive and to grow. Leaves are used to trap light and they vary a lot in shape and size.

The stem (or trunk if it's a tree) holds the whole plant up. It also carries water, food and other goodness around the plant.

SOIL

Soil and **compost** contain important nutrients that plants need to grow. When plants die, they put this goodness back into the soil for new plants to enjoy.

WATER

Just like with humans, water is essential for life on Earth. You'll notice that a plant needs watering if its stem and leaves become droopy.

WARMTH

Plants thrive in the right temperatures and most plants like a little warmth. Only certain plants will survive in extreme conditions, such as intense wind or heat.

WHY DO WE NEED PLANTS?

Plants are the foundation of all life on Earth and they help us in many wonderful ways. They are used for food and medicine, they clean the air we breathe, provide **habitats** for many different animals and are used to make products that we use every day. If you're reading this book on paper, it's made from a tree! So, how many different ways do plants help us?

Plants provide 80 per cent of the food we eat. Most of your favourite meals will have come from plants, such as rice, wheat, potatoes and tomatoes.

For thousands of years, people have turned to plants to relieve aches, pains and ailments. Did you know that a blend of chamomile tea can help to settle an upset tummy?

Many modern materials are made from plants. They are used to produce everything from clothing to materials used to create housing. Most recently, plants can be used to reduce harm to our planet. For example, bamboo is an environmentally friendly alternative to plastic.

Plants are important for providing habitats for many different animals. Did you know the English oak tree provides food and shelter to over 2,000 wildlife species? How many can you see in this picture?

Red squirrel

Woodpecker

Ladybird

Plants are all around us. How many different ways do you use plants in your day?

Barn owl

Red fox

Field mouse

Plants are the first link in most **food chains**. When plants grow, they take in nutrients from the soil. When an animal eats a plant, it takes in the nutrients, using them to live and grow. And when an animal eats another animal, the transfer continues. Without plants, the delicate food chain would break.

IT STARTS WITH A SEED

All living things, including plants, have a **life cycle**.
This usually starts with a seed, which grows into a plant if
it has three important things – light, water and warmth.
With the right amount – not too much or too little – the plant
will continue to grow a taller, thicker stem and more leaves,
and sometimes flowers. The flowers make seeds and
the whole cycle starts again.

1.
Once a plant seed is planted in soil, it will **germinate** (sprout) and start growing little roots. The roots anchor the plant into the soil and allow it to start sucking up water.

2.
Next, little leaves will pop out of the soil on the top of a thin stem. This gives the young plant the height it needs to grow above its neighbours to reach sunlight.

3.
Using soil, water, air and sunlight, the plant begins to make its own food and fuel for growth. This process is called photosynthesis.

4.
The plant will continue to grow a taller and thicker stem and more leaves until it becomes an adult. Depending on the species of plant, this can take anything from days to weeks or years!

5.

After the plant becomes mature, it will start to produce flowers. These flowers are important in a plant's life cycle as this is where the new seeds are made. In other words, the flower is where reproduction happens.

6.

So that plants can make seeds, a sticky substance called pollen usually has to be transferred from one plant to another. This process is called **pollination**. Learn more about pollination on pages 16–17.

7.

In the final stage, the plant's seeds are dispersed (spread to new places) and a new plant life cycle begins. The seeds are usually spread by water, wind and sometimes by animals.

THE POWER OF POLLINATION

Did you know that insects **help plants to grow**? Without them, the natural world as we know it would not exist. This is because insects help to pollinate plants. Flowers contain pollen, which needs to reach other flowers so they can make seeds. The best way for pollen to travel between plants is by insect!

Bee

Moth

1. When a bee visits a flower, the pollen gets stuck to the insect's hairy body.

2. The bee flies off in search of another flower. When it lands, some of the pollen rubs off onto the stigma (female part) of the new flower.

Butterfly

Some insects, such as butterflies, moths and wasps, use their legs or long tongues to pollinate flowers.

3. The pollen fertilises the flower and it is now able to make seeds. The **pollinator** has done its job by spreading pollen to create new plants!

BUILD A BUG HOTEL FOR YOUR POLLINATORS

YOU WILL NEED:

- Wooden palettes
- Sticks
- Stones
- Dead stems
- Pine cones
- Bricks
- Pots of flowers

1. Choose a safe part of the garden where your bug hotel won't be disturbed. Place your first wooden palette on the ground and line bricks around the corners and across the middle. Place your next pallet on top of this and repeat the process until they are all used up.

2. Next, pile up your sticks, stones and stems into different zones, like this picture. You could have a pile of pine cones in one area and a neat stack of bricks in another.

3. Arrange some pots of flowers nearby – this will attract pollinators to come and look around. If they like it, they'll move in!

ALL ABOUT SOIL

Soil is the brown earth that plants grow in and it plays a very important role in supporting life on our planet. The best way to keep your plants happy is to take care of their soil!

Once a seed has sprouted, the soil helps to anchor the plant's roots in the ground. From here, the roots can absorb water, nutrients and minerals from the soil that help the plant to grow.

Soil is teeming with life. Did you know that there are more living things in a handful of soil than there are humans on Earth? Soil is full of tiny living organisms such as plants, fungi, insects and bacteria.

GET TO KNOW YOUR SOIL

Soils vary around the world, but they all contain sand, silt, clay, moisture and air. As a gardener, it's important to get to know your soil. If a plant is from a sandy part of the world and you try growing it in a wet clay soil, it won't be happy! Similarly, a plant from a damp area won't like to grow in a sandy soil.

1. Using a trowel (see pages 24–25), collect a soil sample from your garden. Lay it out on a piece of paper, remove any twiggy bits, then using your trowel, crush the soil so it's as fine as possible.

2. Next, part fill a large jar with the soil sample, cover with water, put the lid on tightly and then give it a good shake before leaving it for at least 24 hours to settle.

3. You should now be able to see the different layers of your soil. The parts of soil are different weights and the heavier ones – like sand – fall to the bottom first. Clay will settle last and even make the top layer quite cloudy for a while, as its tiny particles float in the water.

These organisms have special functions. Worms, for example, are little underground helpers. They munch on things at the soil's surface, then dig tunnels deep down. As they dig, they poop out what they have eaten, which is like a special kind of food for the soil.

19

GETTING STARTED...

ALL KINDS OF GARDENS

Did you know that gardens don't have to be outside?
Whether it's a windowsill or small hanging basket, as long
as there is enough sunlight, shade, moisture and wind,
plants can thrive.

WINDOWSILLS

Many plants love windowsills
because they get plenty of light.
Just keep an eye on the soil to
make sure it doesn't dry out!
Growing plants in containers is
a great activity if you don't have
a lot of outdoor space.

AROUND THE HOUSE

Many plants love living indoors.
There are hundreds of different
varieties of house plants and
vegetables that can easily be
grown in your house.

HANGING BASKET

You don't need a lot of
space to put up a hanging
basket! Some plants can
grow downwards as well
as up and out.

Go for a walk near your home. How many different types of gardens can you spot?

FAMILY GARDEN

If you have a garden, ask an adult if you can use part of it to grow your first plants. It can be helpful to ask for hints and tips about what has grown well there before!

ALLOTMENT

An allotment is a patch of land away from your house that is just for your plants. Often there are also other gardeners at the allotment who can offer you help and advice.

COMMUNITY GARDEN

Community gardens offer local people a place to garden and to make friends. The garden can be a few beds or a huge space, and there is always room for one more helper!

23

TOOLS AT THE READY

There are a few handy tools that can come in useful when tending to your garden. Sometimes you might even be able to make your own tools at home.

SPADE

Spades can be used for larger jobs, such as planting trees and shrubs.

GARDEN HOE

A garden hoe is useful for shaping the soil and pulling up weeds.

KNEELING MAT

It can make your knees hurt if you kneel on hard ground for too long. Try using a kneeling mat – or even an old towel or piece of cardboard.

LABELS

It can be helpful to add labels to your pots or plant beds to help you identify your plants while they're growing.

SECATEURS

Secateurs are garden scissors that are often used to cut small stems and branches.

WHEELBARROW

A wheelbarrow is a useful tool as it helps to transport heavy items around the garden, such as plants or compost.

TROWEL AND FORK

A trowel helps you to dig small, neat holes. If you don't have one, an old wooden spoon will work just fine. A garden fork can be used for breaking up clumps of hard soil and for carefully digging up weeds.

MATTOCK

A mattock is hand tool that can be used for creating holes and removing large roots and rocks.

BUCKET

A bucket or old container can be very useful for collecting weeds, rather than leaving piles around your garden.

WATERING CAN

Your seedlings and plants will need plenty of water to grow. If you don't have a watering can, you can always ask an adult to pierce holes in the lid of an old water bottle.

GARDENING GLOVES

Some plants can be prickly and might graze your hands. It can be helpful to wear special gardening gloves to protect your hands.

RAKE

A rake can be helpful to break up the soil and level the ground.

SEARCHING FOR SEEDS

You can find seeds almost everywhere if you know where to look. Many of the plants we have in the garden or kitchen already contain the seeds we need to grow the same plant. If it's the right time of year, you can plant the seeds straight away, or you can store them in a labelled envelope for next year.

FROM THE KITCHEN

Lots of **fruits** have seeds inside them, from apple pips to avocado stones. For the best chance of growing kitchen seeds, choose organic fruit and vegetables to harvest from.

Apples

Pumpkins

Peppers

Avocados

Tomatoes

IN THE GARDEN

There are many different seeds that you can find in your garden. Did you know that you can find seeds inside sunflower heads? Collect seeds on a dry day and leave them in a cool place indoors.

BUYING SEEDS

You can also buy seeds from a supermarket, garden centre or online seed shop. Specialist shops have lots of information about what plants can be grown in particular conditions.

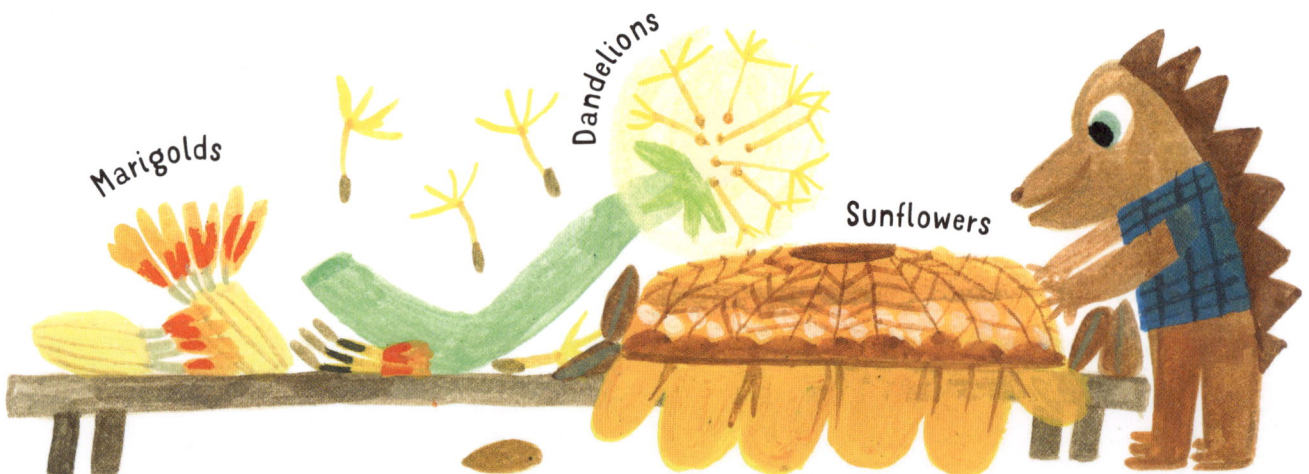

Dandelions

Marigolds

Sunflowers

HOW TO SOW SEEDS

Learning how to sow seeds is an essential skill for any gardener. Seeds don't need large containers to begin with — you can start growing new seeds in small pots before transferring them to your garden. You can use anything from egg boxes to yoghurt pots or even toilet roll tubes!

YOU WILL NEED:

- **Any small reused containers** (washed) — ask an adult to remove the labels

- **Compost**

- **Cress seeds**

- **Fruit punnet or plastic bottle** (cut into two halves)

- **Water**

1. Fill each pot with compost. Ask an adult to pierce drainage holes in the bottom.

2. Sprinkle cress seeds into the pot, add a little compost and water well.

3. Cover the seeds with a fruit punnet or plastic bottle, and place on a windowsill or in a warm spot. Give them water each day.

4. The cress seeds will start to sprout in just a few days, and a few days after that you can harvest and eat them!

CARING FOR YOUR PLANTS

Taking care of your plants may seem tricky at first, but with a little patience and care, your plants will be healthy and happy. Here are some helpful tips all gardeners must know.

WATERING

Plants need water to survive, but different plants require different amounts of water. It's important to check the instructions that come with each plant – over watering or under watering can be harmful.

FEEDING

Just like us, plants sometimes need extra help to grow strong and healthy. You can feed your plants with organic **fertilisers** to give them the nutrients they need.

WEEDING

Weeds are plants that grow where we don't want them to. While some weeds are harmless, others can overcrowd your garden plants. To keep your garden looking neat and tidy, remove unwanted plants regularly by pulling them out by the roots.

PRUNING

Pruning is the process of cutting away overgrown branches or stems, especially to encourage growth. It is an essential garden task that keeps your plants healthy and tidy.

LIGHT AND SHELTER

Some plants like a lot of sunshine, while others prefer shade. It's important to position your plants in the right place so that they get the right amount of light. Shelter from wind, rain and frost may also be needed.

FIRST AID

Just like people, plants can sometimes get sick. If you notice that your plant is wilting or the leaves are turning brown, it may be a sign of a problem. Some solutions include changing the amount of water or light the plant is getting, adding fertiliser or compost, or removing any damaged parts of the plant.

REPOTTING

When you notice roots poking out of the bottom of the pot, your plant needs repotting. Choose a pot that is a few centimetres bigger and your plant will be happy. Start repotting during a warm part of the day and handle your plant as little as possible. Remember to water your plant when it's settled into its new home!

SOWING WITH THE SEASONS

Gardeners have to grow along with the **seasons** – sowing seeds at particular times of the year to fit in with each plant's life cycle. But there are always ways to extend the season and bend the rules a little. For example, growing certain seeds indoors to give them a head start before spring comes.

SPRING

Spring is the perfect time to prepare your garden and to sow your seeds. It starts to feel warmer and sunnier during spring, and existing plants start to grow. You'll also notice birds singing and insects buzzing around. Nature is waking up...

WINTER

The coldest months of the year can be tough on nature, but many plants are well adapted to survive. Now is the time to think about what has worked well in your garden and what you'd like to plant next year. You can also start growing some plants indoors to give them a head start before spring.

SUMMER

It's time to harvest your summer crops! The summer sunshine and showers can cause your garden – both the plants you want and the weeds you don't – to grow wild. Along with juicy new plants come hungry mini beasts, so keep an eye out for garden visitors!

AUTUMN

As the air gets cooler, flowers drop their petals and some trees lose their leaves. It's time to tidy up, harvest the last of the early autumn crops and protect your plants before the cold winter begins. For example, you can position sensitive plants under large evergreen trees to shelter them from the worst of the weather.

WELCOME WILDLIFE

Wildlife gardening can be great way to help to protect the natural world. Gardens are a safe haven for many different kinds of creatures – from bees to butterflies, birds, hedgehogs and even frogs. Your garden is a mini **ecosystem** right on your doorstep!

GROW THE RIGHT PLANTS

It's important to choose plants that will benefit your local wildlife. Chamomile is often found in the United Kingdom because it helps to provide food and shelter for the animals that live there, such as mice and other small mammals.

BUG HOTEL

Insects are important pollinators in your garden. A bug hotel (see page 17) provides a safe and warm place for bugs, such as bees, to return to once they've foraged for food and water and are in need of a rest.

LOG PILE BENCH

Some bugs – such as beetles, spiders and woodlice – love the shade and dampness found underneath logs. If your log is large enough, you could even use it as a bench, so it helps your local wildlife and gives you a lovely place to sit and enjoy your garden.

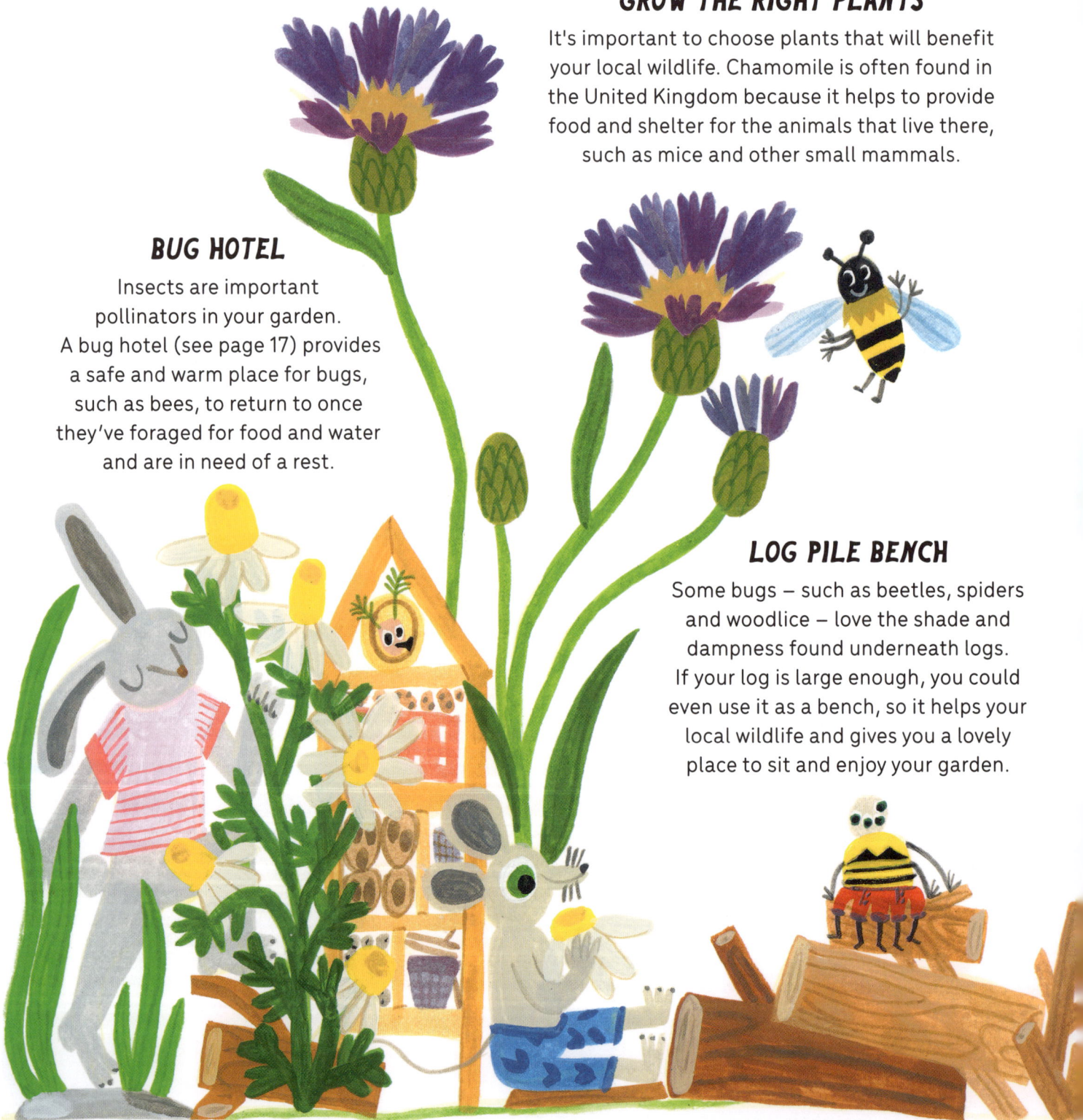

BIRD FEEDERS

When birds have babies in spring, it's important to support them by leaving out extra food. You can make fat balls by mixing lard and seeds together, put out feeders of seeds and nuts, and leave out any berries or fruit that you no longer want.

BIRD HOUSES

As well as sharing food, you can help birds by putting out nesting materials, including twigs, leaves, dry grass, feathers, plant fluff, moss and bark strips.

WATERY WONDERS

Water is an important part of a wildlife garden. By adding a bird bath or small pond, you can provide drinking water for wildlife and attract new species to your garden. Make sure to keep the water fresh and clean to prevent the spread of disease.

It's amazing to watch wildlife thrive in your garden. Can you see how different creatures interact with the plant life and the features you've added? Welcoming wildlife is a great way to connect with nature, learn about the world around you and help you feel happy!

GARDEN FOES

Sometimes your garden might be visited by some not so welcome wildlife visitors – munching their way through your plants and obliterating weeks of hard work. Rather than using harmful chemical **pesticides**, there are some natural ways you can discourage any unexpected visitors to your garden.

ENCOURAGE BENEFICIAL ANIMALS

You can control pest populations naturally by encouraging beneficial creatures, such as ladybirds, wasps, hoverflies, birds and frogs, in your garden. Try planting flowers that attract these insects, making a bug hotel or adding a bird feeder.

PEST REPELLENTS

To repel insects, you can make an organic pest spray using a mixture of water, garlic, onion and chilli.

PROTECT PLANTS

You can cover your plants with netting to stop birds swooping down for a tasty snack.

KEEP AN EYE OUT FOR PESTS

Slugs and snails can eat a whole batch of seedlings overnight. You can try adding a barrier, such as gravel, so they find it more difficult to slither across. Remember to check your pots every day for hiding snails – gently picking them up and putting them in another part of your garden.

PLANTS THAT HELP OTHER PLANTS

Did you know that certain plants can deter or encourage insects to your garden? Growing particular plants together can also aid pollination, prevent disease and even keep pest numbers down. This is called **companion gardening**.

The strong smell of French marigolds deters the pest whitefly when grown with tomatoes.

When planted near strawberries, the borage flower attracts pollinators and can enhance the strawberries' flavour.

Onions, garlic and leeks deter pests from carrot and parsnip plants.

Nasturtiums are so tasty that slugs, snails and other nibblers are drawn to them rather than your plants, so it can be helpful to plant extra as a decoy.

BUILD A COMPOST HEAP

Gardeners often improve the quality of their soil by adding compost – a nutrient-rich mixture that is made from organic materials, such as leaves, paper and food scraps. You can buy compost at your local garden centre or you can even make it yourself! With the right conditions, you can make a natural compost that helps your plants to grow.

YOU WILL NEED:

- **Green matter** (leaves, lawn clippings, weeds, fruits and vegetable scraps from the kitchen, coffee grounds and tea bags)
- **Brown material** (dried twigs, wood chips, fallen leaves, straw, sawdust, card and paper)
- **Spade or trowel**
- **Water**

1. Start by mixing one part of your green matter to two parts brown matter together. Add two spadefuls of soil from your garden to the mix.

2. Turn your pile once a week to let more air in. If it feels like it's drying out, add a little water. If you keep up this routine, you should have a nice compost to use in your garden in about two months.

3. Once your compost heap is ready, you can sift out the finest compost and use it when repotting container plants. Any larger twigs can either go into the next heap or be put onto a garden log pile for wildlife.

Perfect! Now your compost is prepared and you're ready to get growing...

LET'S GROW FRUIT AND VEG!

GROWING FOOD

Gardening for flavour is a fun and rewarding way to ensure that
you are eating the most nutritious, delicious produce possible.
Did you know that there are many edible roots, stems and
leaves that you can grow in your garden?

FRUIT

Apples, grapes and strawberries are
fruits, but would you have guessed
that cucumbers, tomatoes, pumpkins
and peppers are also fruits?

LEAVES

We eat lots of leaves! From
lettuce in salads to cooked
cabbage, kale crisps and spinach,
leaves make up a tasty chunk of
the food on our plates.

SEEDS

Certain plants grow their seeds
inside pods and some of the tastiest
seeds come from peas and beans.
You can pop them out of their pods
and enjoy eating them raw or cooked.

FLOWERS

Nasturtiums are edible flowers, but did you know that broccoli and cauliflower have flowers, too? They are harvested before their yellow flowers bloom.

Try tasting the plants listed on this page. Are they crunchy or soft, sweet or sour, watery or solid?

STEMS

Rhubarb, potatoes and asparagus plants all have edible stems. Rhubarb stems are sour, but are often cooked with sugar and added to pies and other desserts.

ROOTS

Carrots, radishes and beetroot are all grown underground because they're actually the roots of the plant!

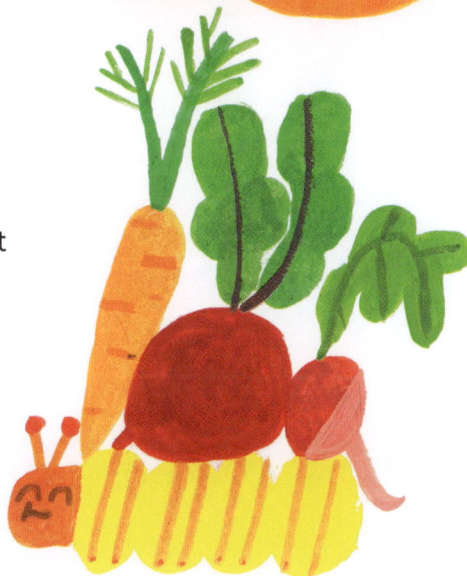

BULBS

Onions and garlic are bulbs – the part of the plant that stores energy. If onions and garlic are planted for long enough, they would grow stems, leaves and even flowers!

MAKE A PEA TEEPEE

Fresh peas taste very different to frozen peas, and are delicious when eaten straight from the pod or cooked. The more peas you pick from your plant, the more peas will grow!

YOU WILL NEED:

- A large container or plant pot
- Spade or trowel
- Compost
- Pea plants
- 5-6 canes or long, sturdy sticks
- An elastic band or string
- Plant food
- Water

1.

Fill a large pot with compost and position it in a sunny spot.

2.

Dig small holes and add your pea plants around the edges, spaced apart.

3.

Next to each plant, carefully push a cane or stick into the compost. Hold the tops of the canes together and secure them with an elastic band or string, so the canes form a teepee shape. You may need an adult to help with this.

4.

Water your plants each day and feed them once a week. As they start to grow, gently help the thin tendrils to wind around the canes.

5.

You will notice small white flowers growing on the stems — this is where your pea pods will soon appear.

6.

When you can feel peas inside the pea pods, they are ready to be picked!

GROW HANGING STRAWBERRIES

Strawberries are wonderful fruits to grow in your first garden – they're easy to grow and they taste delicious. If you don't have much space, hanging pots are perfect. It's best to grow strawberry plants in spring and then you can harvest the fruits during the warm summer months.

YOU WILL NEED:

- **A hanging pot** (use a hanging basket or an old colander with some string attached)
- **Compost**
- **Strawberry plants**
- **Fertiliser**
- **Netting**
- **Water**

1.

Add a little compost to your hanging pot, then a strawberry plant and a little more compost, if needed. The roots and part of the stem should be completely covered. You should add two to three strawberry plants to your hanging pot.

2.

Ask an adult to help you to hang your pot using the string. Make sure it's in a sunny spot.

3.

Water your plants every day, unless it rains! You can also give the plant fertiliser if it is struggling to grow – ask an adult to help you with this.

4.

As the leaves grow, white flowers will appear. From the middle of the flower, you'll notice something that looks like a tiny yellow strawberry.

5.

Once your strawberries start to grow, it's a good idea to cover them with a net to stop birds eating them.

6.

When the strawberries have turned completely red, you can pick them. Wash and eat them on the same day for a delicious burst of flavour.

GROW A CANNED HERB GARDEN

Herbs are small plants that we add to meals to give them extra flavour. Many herbs are easy to grow and they are perfectly suited to a sunny windowsill, so there's no risk of any garden bugs having a midnight feast on them!

YOU WILL NEED:

- **Tin cans** (washed) – ask an adult to remove the lids and labels
- **Acrylic paints and a brush**
- **Compost**
- **Herb seeds** (mint, basil and parsley)
- **A plate**
- **Water**

1. Ask an adult to pierce drainage holes into each tin can.

Basil

2. Paint your cans with lovely patterns. Leave the cans to dry for 24 hours.

4. Leave the cans on a sunny windowsill and water every few days. After a week or two, you'll see small shoots growing.

3. Fill the cans with compost. Next, sprinkle seeds in each can, and cover with a little compost. Water the seeds, then put the cans on a plate so that any excess water drains onto it.

Parsley

Mint

Taste each leaf. Can you think of describing words for the taste and smell?

5. After a month, your herbs should be big enough to harvest as and when you need them.

GROW A BUCKET OF TOMATOES

Tomato plants are easy to grow, and it's great to watch them get bigger by the day. There are so many varieties of tomatoes to choose from – from tomatoes with red, yellow or orange fruit, to small cherries and large beefsteaks.

YOU WILL NEED:

- A bucket
- Decoration for your bucket (optional)
- Spade or trowel
- Compost
- Plant food
- A tomato plant
- A cane or sturdy stick
- Water

1. Ask an adult to add drainage holes to the bottom of your bucket. Decorate the pot as you wish.

2. Fill your bucket almost to the brim with compost.

3. Dig a small hole in the middle and add your tomato plant. Add more compost until it is level and your plant is sturdy.

4. Put your bucket in a sunny spot in your garden. It's a good idea to add a cane or stick that can support the tomato plant as it gets taller.

5. Water the plant every day and once it starts to grow, cut off any side shoots. This ensures the plant puts all its energy into growing the main plant.

6. In a few weeks, you'll notice small stems of yellow flowers, called trusses. Before long, tiny tomatoes will appear from the flowers. Make sure to feed them with plant food once every two weeks.

7. When the tomato fruits turn red, yellow or orange, you can pick and enjoy them straight from the plant.

LET'S GROW PLANTS!

GROWING PLANTS

Gardens are beautiful, tranquil spaces that everyone can enjoy. From towering trees to sweet-smelling flowers, there are many different kinds of plants you can grow. Take care to choose plants that grow at different times of the year, so there's always something to discover in your garden.

SWEET-SMELLING PLANTS

If you love sweet-smelling gardens, you can choose plants like lavender, honeysuckle, jasmine, gardenia, sweet pea and viburnum. These plants have flowers that produce nectar with a wonderful scent that can attract pollinators, such as bees, butterflies and moths, to your garden.

SCENTED LEAVES

Flowers aren't the only part of plants that can smell good. Some plants have leaves that are also strongly scented, such as the curry plant, thyme and pelargoniums. You can rub these leaves gently between your fingers to release their delicious fragrance.

How many different types of plants are growing in your garden? Do they have an interesting smell or texture to them?

TREES AND SHRUBS

Planting trees and shrubs can be a great way to enhance your garden – offering shade and a natural windbreak from the weather. Planting trees is also a great way to attract wildlife, giving them space to shelter and to feed.

COLOURFUL PLANTS

There are many different plants that are known for their colourful flowers or leaves. From tulips to fuchsias, you will never be short of colour to add to your garden.

DIFFERENT TEXTURES

Gardens can be full of delightful things to touch and feel. You can incorporate plants with different textures, such as velvety or furry leaves, as well as feathery ferns.

GROW A WELLY BOOT SUNFLOWER

This striking sun-like flower is a great addition to any garden because it's easy to grow, bees and other insects love it, and birds can feast on the seeds. It can also be fun to have a sunflower-growing competition with a friend or family member to see how high they can grow!

YOU WILL NEED:

- An old welly boot
- Compost
- Sunflower seeds
- Canes or sturdy sticks
- String
- Water

1. Ask an adult to add drainage holes into the bottom of the welly boot. They may find it easier to remove the insole first.

2. Fill the boot with compost.

3. Poke a small hole in the compost with your finger and add a seed.

4. Cover the seed with compost and water, and place the boot in a sunny spot.

5. Water the plant a little every day, and after a week or two a shoot will appear.

6. Now the fun starts! Watch the stem grow taller and taller, and then the flower head will appear.

7. Push a cane into the compost and loosely tie the stem to it. This is to stop the plant falling over and snapping.

8. Once the plant has died, you can leave the seed head outside for birds, mice and other small animals to enjoy.

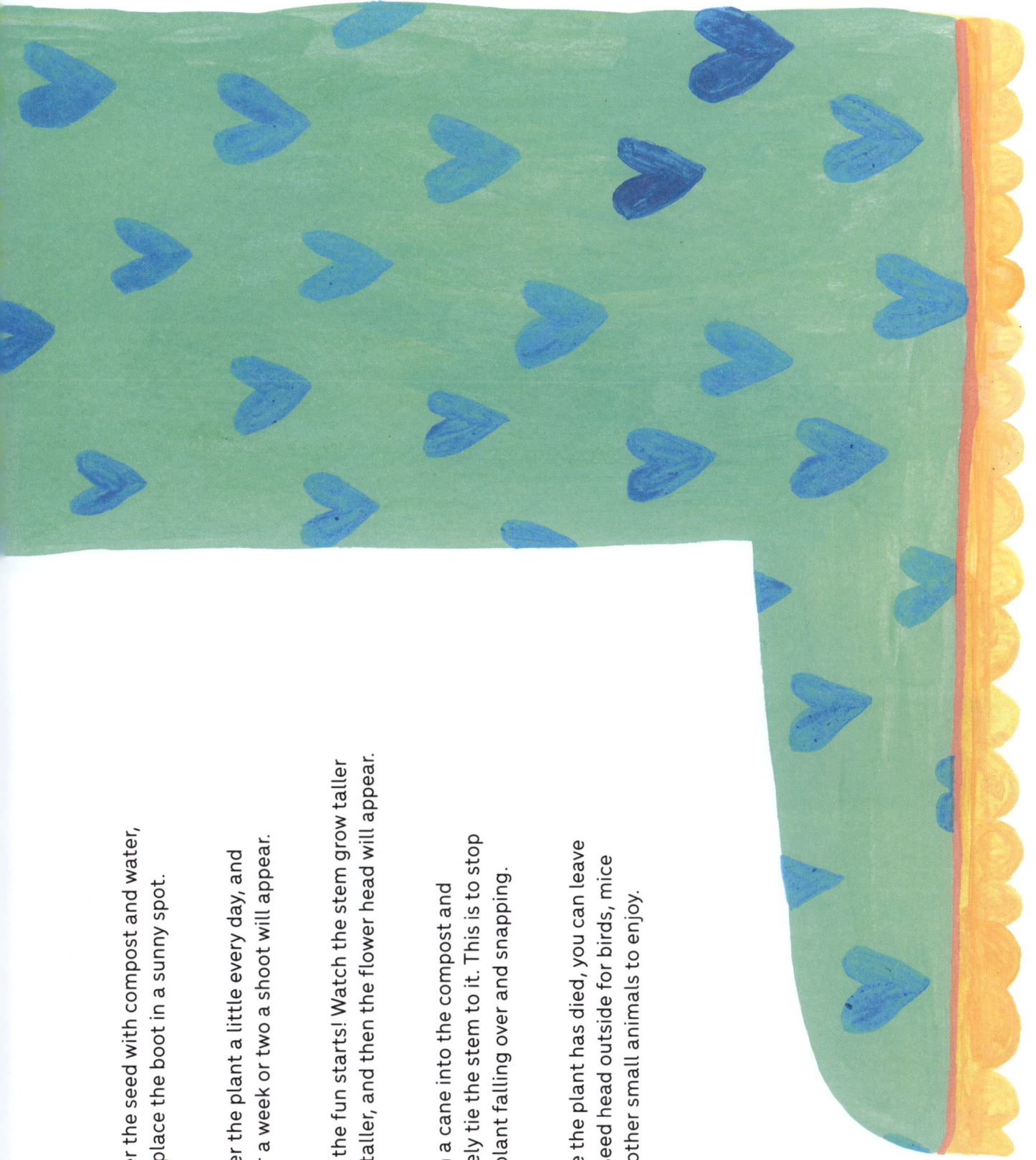

GROW CUPS OF NASTURTIUMS

Did you know that you can eat the petals from certain flowers? Nasturtiums are bright and colourful, and they taste a bit peppery! You can add them to a salad for a burst of extra flavour.

YOU WILL NEED:

- Old cups or mugs
- Gravel
- Compost
- Nasturtium seeds
- Water

1. In the bottom of each cup, add a layer of gravel. This is to allow the water to drain away from the roots because the cups do not have any drainage holes.

2. Fill each cup with compost.

3. Poke a couple of holes in the compost and drop in the seeds.

5. After a week or two, the seeds will start to shoot. Make sure to keep giving them water, little and often.

4. Cover with a little extra compost and add water. Be careful not to soak the compost – remember the water can't drain away as well.

6. In a few more weeks, flowers will appear. You can harvest them whenever you like. If any die on the plant, just pull them off and a new one will grow in its place.

CREATE A MINI WORLD

In 1829, a **botanist** called Nathaniel Bagshaw Ward noticed a fern growing in a jar on his windowsill. The ferns he'd tried to grow in his own garden had died because of the polluted city air, but here was one protected in its own 'mini world'. Inspired by this discovery, Ward invented the terrarium – a miniature garden protected inside a glass container. Terrariums are still popular to this day.

YOU WILL NEED:

- **A homemade cardboard funnel**
- **A large jar**
- **Gravel or pumice**
- **Activated charcoal**
- **Compost**
- **Plants** (minature palm trees, miniature orchids, small spider plants)
- **Stones for the soil surface** (optional)
- **Water**

1. Use the funnel to make a layer of gravel or pumice at the bottom of your container.

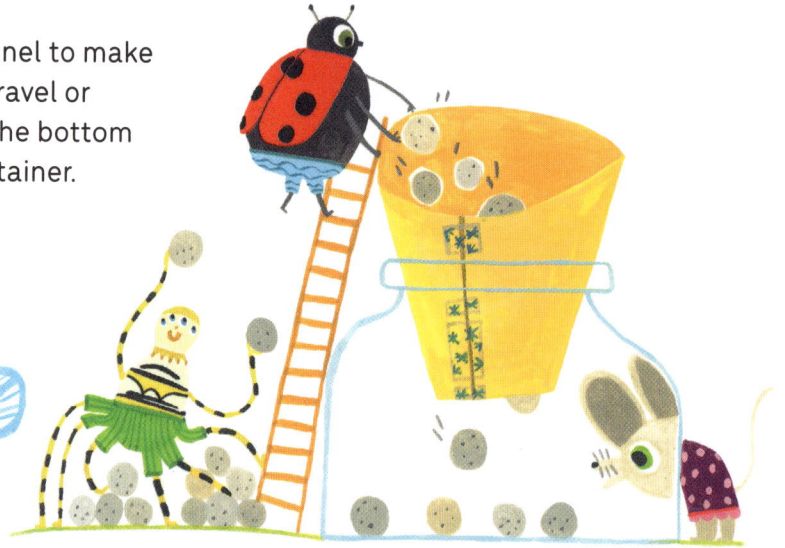

2. Scatter a thin layer of activated charcoal over the gravel or pumice. Next add a layer of compost (at least deep enough for the depth of the plant roots).

3. Add some water so the compost is damp, not wet.

4. Water your plants before removing them from their pots and then lower them into their new positions.

5. Add stones to the surface of the compost and close the lid. Position your terrarium in a bright spot away from direct sunlight.

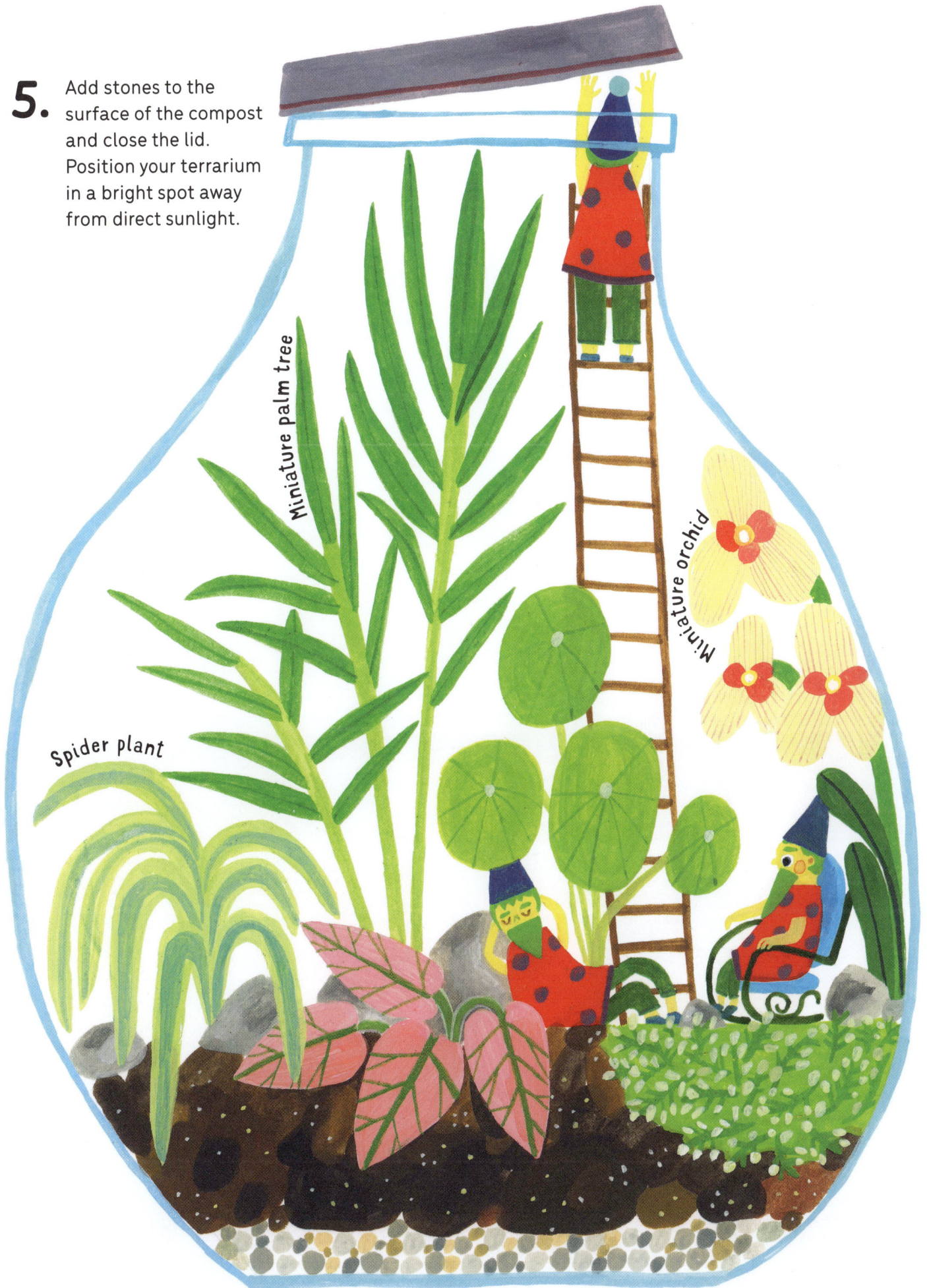

Miniature palm tree

Miniature orchid

Spider plant

GROW A SUCCULENT FROM A LEAF

Succulents are fascinating plants that are able store water in their leaves or stems. Because of this special ability, succulents can live in very dry places where other plants would die. These little plants are easy to care for and have become very popular house plants. But did you know that you can grow a succulent from a leaf?

YOU WILL NEED:

- A succulent plant (sedums or echeverias)
- A container for the leaves
- Compost
- Plant pots
- Water

1. Pluck several leaves from the plant stem — gently twisting the entire leaf off at the base.

2. Once you've plucked your leaves, it's important to let them dry before you do anything else. Depending on the amount of heat and sunlight in the room, you will need to leave the leaf for one to three days, so it can scab over.

3. Lay the leaves in a container on top of some compost. Take care to water the soil regularly to ensure the leaves do not dry out.

4. It takes some time for new roots to form on succulent leaves, but you can expect to see some results within two to three weeks. As your new plants start to grow, make sure to keep the roots covered with compost, or they'll dry out and your plants will probably stop growing.

5. Wait until your new plant is at least 2.5 centimetres in diameter before repotting it. After your succulent is settled in its new home, make sure you water it once a week to ensure it keeps growing. That's it! You have created a brand new plant.

GLOSSARY

BOTANIST
A scientist who studies plants.

CARBON DIOXIDE
A gas released by the burning of coal, natural gas, oil and wood that traps heat in the atmosphere.

COMPANION GARDENING
Planting plants that like growing in the same conditions next to each other.

COMPOST
A nutrient-rich mixture that is made from organic materials, such as leaves, paper and food scraps.

ECOSYSTEM
All the living things found in a particular area along with all the factors that affect them (such as the weather, type of soil or other living things).

FERTILISER
A chemical that is added to the soil that helps plants to grow.

FLOWER
The part of a plant where the male and female parts are found.

FOOD CHAIN
The way of depicting organisms showing the order in which they are eaten.

FRUIT
The part of a flowering plant that contains seeds.

GERMINATE
The process by which a plant grows from a seed.

HABITAT
An animal or plant's natural environment.

INSECT
A creature that has a body with three sections that are protected by a shell.

LEAF
The part of a plant that catches sunlight and makes food during photosynthesis.

NUTRIENTS

Chemicals or substances that help a living thing grow (such as minerals in the soil).

OXYGEN

A colourless gas in the air. All living things need it to survive. Humans breathe oxygen in from the air.

PESTICIDE

A substance used to get rid of plants, animals and fungi that are unwanted. Overuse of these chemicals can be harmful to the environment.

PHOTOSYNTHESIS

The process by which plants make their own food using sunlight energy, water, carbon dioxide and nutrients.

POLLINATION

The process where pollen is transferred between flowers, resulting in seed production.

POLLINATOR

Animals that pollinate a plant, including birds and bees.

ROOTS

Roots help to hold the plant in one place and collect water.

SEASONS

Seasons are periods of the year marked by specific weather conditions. The four seasons are spring, summer, autumn and winter.

SOIL

Soil is the loose upper layer of the Earth's surface where plants grow.

SEED

A case that contains everything needed to grow a new plant.

STEM

The part of a plant that grows upwards from the seed. Buds, leaves, flowers and branches grow out from it.

VEGETABLE

The part of a plant that is edible. Vegetables include leaves, stalks, flowers, fruit, seeds, roots and bulbs.

ABOUT THE AUTHOR

Michael Holland is a London-based freelance nature educator and writer. As a child, he was inspired by Keith Mossman's *The Pip Book,* which started his hobby of growing plants and appreciating the natural world. He spent much of his childhood exploring the woods and landscapes of Great Britain before studying Ecology at university. Michael's previous books include *I Ate Sunshine for Breakfast, Smart Animals* and *A Jungle In Your Living Room.*

ABOUT THE ILLUSTRATOR

Maria Dek studied art at the Academy of Fine Arts in Warsaw and University of the Arts London. She is based in Bialowieza, Poland, in the oldest forest in Europe. Her previous books include *A Walk in the Forest* and *When I Am Big.* Maria uses the traditional technique of gouache to create her charming, joyful illustrations.